Look closely among bright fall foliage and you might find a leafy look-alike hiding in plain sight.

WHAT IN THE WORLD?

A CLOSER LOOK

JULIE VOSBURGH AGNONE

NATIONAL GEOGRAPHIC KiDS

WASHINGTON, D.C.

HOW TO PLAY

YOUR BRAIN ON PUZZLES! You rely on your sense of vision and your brain to understand the world around you. But as amazing as your eyes are, the pictures they send your brain are quirky: They're upside down, backward, and two-dimensional! Your brain automatically flips the images from your retinas right side up and combines the views from each eye into a three-dimensional image. No wonder picture puzzles can be tough. But puzzles help strengthen your visual perception and cognitive skills, so think of this book as a workout for your brain.

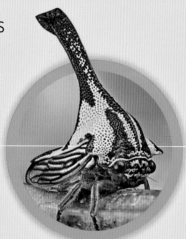

WHAT IN THE WORLD?

Patterns, colors, and shapes help you identify things. The photos in these games show only partial views of animals and objects, which means your brain has to do some heavy lifting to identify what you're seeing. Sound like a challenge that will help bulk up your brain?
HOW TO PLAY: Use photos, written clues, and scrambled words to find the answers.

HOW TO PLAY: Study the images to decide what is real, and what is actually fake!

TAKE A LOOK!

Puzzles like these require you to spend time finding objects, and that helps stretch your attention and memory. While you're searching among a wild jumble of objects for a pig or a circus ticket, you're building brainpower by exercising your concentration skills.
HOW TO PLAY: Find all of the items on the list.

REAL OR FAKE?

Is seeing always believing? With modern technology, you can never be too sure. On these pages you'll find some truly incredible images of amazing things that really exist in our world—but you'll also find some that are a little too outrageous to be true. You have to put on your thinking cap and be super skeptical of these sneaky shots.

UP CLOSE

Scientists using powerful microscopes can zoom in to reveal stunning details and unseen worlds. The scanning electron microscope (SEM for short) can magnify objects 500,000 times. You may think you're seeing aliens from another planet, so you'll have to flex your logical-thinking muscles to solve these puzzles.

HOW TO PLAY: Match each extreme close-up in the top row with an image in the bottom row.

HIDDEN ANIMALS

Animals often have coloring and patterns that help them blend in with their surroundings and keep them safe from predators. Called camouflage, this trick enables some animals to hide in plain sight! You'll practice attention to detail and visual discrimination strengths with these puzzlers.

HOW TO PLAY: Find the hidden animals in their natural habitats.

OPTICAL ILLUSION

These tricky pics are designed to fool your eyes and brain! Some optical illusions appear to be one thing, but also look like another. This trick often works from a particular viewpoint, and it's all about perception: how your brain interprets conflicting information you're seeing.

HOW TO PLAY: Take a second look at the image. Is there another way to interpret these wacky photos?

DOUBLE TAKE

Two seemingly similar photographs filled with multicolored objects present a challenge to find ten differences between the two images. You will use your visual discrimination—the ability to pick out differences and similarities— as well as exercise concentration and short-term memory.

HOW TO PLAY: Find all of the differences between the two photographs.

MORE CHALLENGES

Ready for the next level? This section offers bonus activities that will expand your brain and build your mental fitness, which boosts your ability to think and learn. It's like having a personal trainer for your brain. Fun activities will extend your cognitive brain skills by relating the puzzling pictures in this book to the real world. Create your own cool optical illusions, test your short- and long-term memory, and see how fast your brain can process exciting new challenges!

Everyone's brain works differently, so don't worry if some of the puzzles are difficult at first. They get easier with practice! Answers are on pages 44–46.

This flashy flock is pretty in pink on a lake in Kenya, Africa.

MAINFGOLS

IDASLN

If you're at sea trying to recognize this, you're in the right place.

OLRAC EREF

This may look like a rocky lunar landscape, but it's very much alive!

The sun casts shadows that double this dromedary desert caravan.

SMECAL

Try not to get lost in this dense deciduous place. Can't see the answer for the trees?

REFSOT

SEEGBICR

These floating frozen floes are drifters in the extremes.

PUTLI FESLID

It may be hard to see the plot, but this pretty perspective is a patchwork of petals.

Maybe it's full of hot air, but this has lofty aspirations.

THO-RIA OLABLON

Herd of these African natives? They travel everywhere together and carry their trunks with them.

SPLEENHTA

BIRD'S-EYE VIEW **WHAT IN THE WORLD?**

REAL OR FAKE? BIZARRE ANIMAL BODIES

Yikes! Have you ever encountered any of these unusual creatures? You may wonder about the insect's tall appendage or the spikes on the snake's head. And what are those big bumps on that reptile's face? Have you seen a giant crab climb a tree? It may be difficult to believe that only *one* of these animals is a fake. See if you can figure out which of these images are real and which is the fake!

Fun Fact!
A giant **coconut crab** weighs up to **40 pounds** (18 kg) and can **crack open a coconut** with its pincers.

TAKE A LOOK!
GALÁPAGOS ISLANDS

< FIND THESE ITEMS IN THE GALÁPAGOS ISLANDS. >

- 3 iguanas
- 6 crabs
- 1 penguin
- 3 snorkelers
- 3 cactus trees
- 3 sea lions
- 1 Galápagos tortoise
- 4 blue-footed boobies
- 4 flamingos
- 1 pair of sunglasses

MOTH CATERPILLAR

SNOWFLAKE

DAMSELFLY

The top row of photographs shows extreme close-ups of the same things that appear in the second row, but in a different order. Match the magnified images with the named objects.

4

5

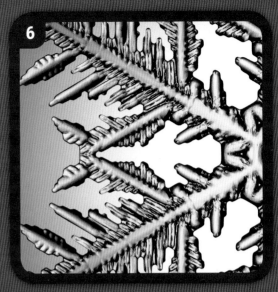

6

PINECONE

CROWNED CRANE

CHAMELEON

MAGNIFICATION **UP** CLOSE

FROGFISH

LEAF BUTTERFLY

SEAHORSE

LICHEN SPIDER

FROG

HAWKSBILL TURTLE

HIDDEN ANIMALS CAMOUFLAGE

At first glance you might think you're seeing the impossible—a two-headed zebra! But look carefully. It's actually two animals, but their converging stripe patterns and the camera angle make it hard to see where one zebra ends and the other begins! Find out more on page 44.

The spectacular array of soft corals and brilliant fishes in a coral reef near Fiji in the South Pacific resembles an underwater garden.

Fun Fact! The **biggest living structure** on Earth is **Australia's Great Barrier Reef.**

The ultimate light
show is quite a sight
on a starry night.

RORNEHTN
SHIGLT

TELICHROPE

It looks like this man-made medical mover is on a mission.

TAB

What flaps and flies, but is neither bird nor insect? You might go batty trying to guess.

This dotty lady takes off on transparent wings.

BLAUDGY

The sky's the limit for this high flier equipped with a tail and tether.

TIKE

GHAN GERLDI

This guy hangs tight, gliding like a butterfly from amazing heights.

PEASC TATSINO

For a place surrounded by space, this way station offers only cramped quarters.

A dazzling display of noise and light resembles a thunderstorm on a summer night.

KISFRWEOR

Some squawk, others talk! This pretty parrot loves life in tropical treetops.

CAMWA

LOOK UP WHAT IN THE WORLD?

< FIND THESE ITEMS IN THE BARNYARD. >

2 cats	3 hoses
4 sheep	4 mice
11 geese	3 hay bales
7 pigs	4 pails
1 donkey	1 goat

REAL OR FAKE? BIZARRE ANIMAL BODIES

Whoa! These crazy critters could be contenders for the animal extremes awards. But do furry birds, antelopes with impossibly long necks, poodle-like insects, and reptiles with flexible tongues really exist? It's up to you to determine what's real and what's fake.

Fun Fact! A **chameleon** can shoot its **sticky tongue** more than **one and a half times** its body length to zap prey at **lightning speed.**

1

2

3

GREEN TREE PYTHON

MORPHO BUTTERFLY

SEA STAR

Here are more mind-boggling magnifications to mix up your brain! Match the extreme close-up images on the top row with the named objects.

4

5

6

SNOW PEAS

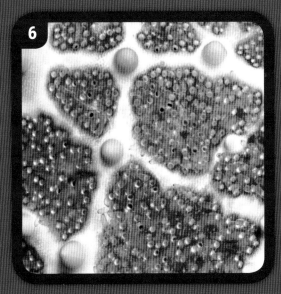

PHEASANT

ELEPHANT

MAGNIFICATION **UP** CLOSE

CARPET SHARK

CATERPILLAR

CRAB SPIDER

ORCHID MANTIS

CRINOID SHRIMP

WHITE-TAILED DEER

HIDDEN ANIMALS CAMOUFLAGE

This optical illusion might make you think a young sea turtle is giving its lazy twin a piggyback ride. But it's really just one turtle! This funny photo is an example of a phenomenon called "total internal reflection," which creates a mirror image at the ocean's surface. Read more about how photographers use this effect on page 45.

TAKE A LOOK!

< FIND THESE CIRCUS ITEMS. >

- 7 tickets
- 3 blue balloons
- 3 tubs of popcorn
- 10 cotton candies
- 1 gum machine
- 3 stuffed animals
- 2 hamsters
- 4 hats
- 2 jugglers
- 6 pigeons

Open-air markets in Morocco offer a variety of goods—from spices to jewelry to handmade crafts, such as painted plates, carved animal statues, and clay cooking pots.

Fun Fact!

There's no need for price tags at a **Moroccan souk,** or grand bazaar. **Bargaining is expected,** and buyers and sellers are supposed to **haggle over the cost of every item.**

DOUBLE TAKE

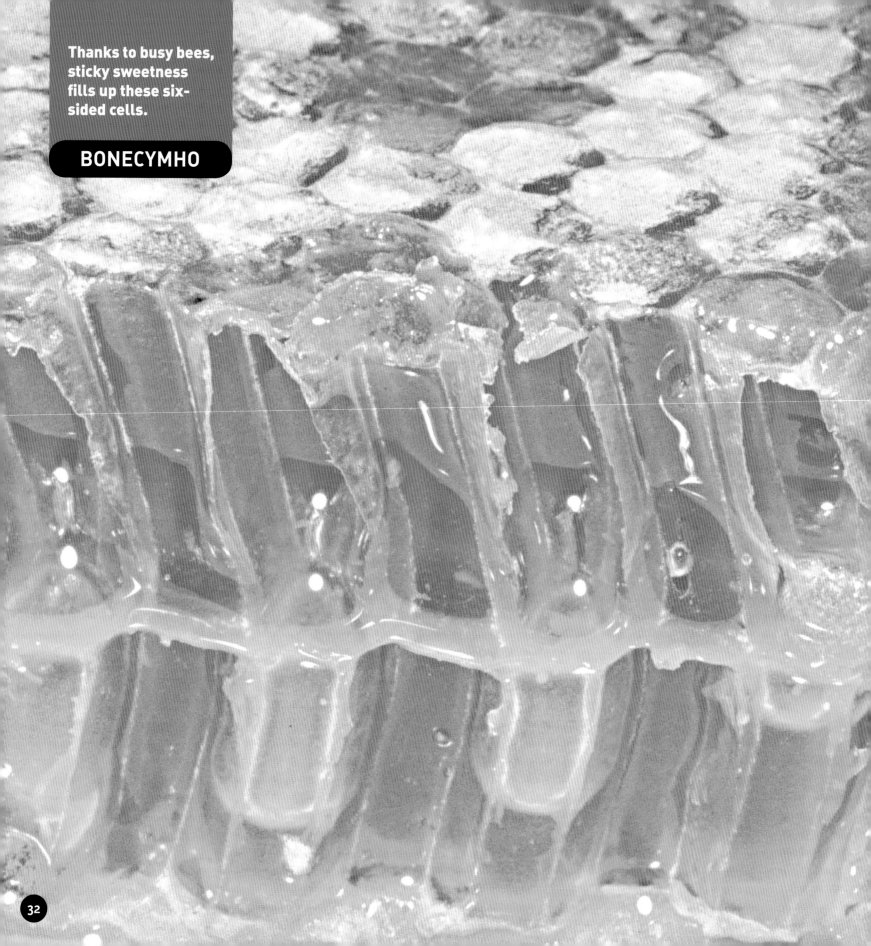

TUBFYTLRE

This transformer has the amazing ability to change from walker to flyer.

NORC

"Oh, shucks" may sound corny, but you're sure to find crispy kernels inside.

If you're used to being served in court, this ball's for you.

NITSEN LABL

Contrary to popular opinion, this amphibian is never slimy, but it's certainly sneaky!

KNASE

NAYCAR

This yellow fellow may sing you to sleep if you care for your pet properly.

FUNRWESLOS

This sunny bunch faces up and stands tall.

This garden creeper moves at such a slow pace you might call it sluggish.

LUGS

Maybe a taste of this will turn you into a sourpuss, but lots of folks love this tart citrus.

OELMN

YELLOWS WHAT IN THE WORLD?

An airplane landing over a highway, an upside-down athlete, a kangaroo adopting a teddy bear, and animals jumping over each other are all possible, right? The world is in constant motion, and wacky things are happening all the time, but maybe some of the activities you're seeing are just a little *too* wacky. Tune in to your real-o-meter and see if you can identify which of these activities are real and which are fake.

Fun Fact!

A **zedonk** is a cross between a male zebra and a female donkey.

FEATHER STAR CLINGFISH

COYOTE

GREEN TREE FROG

EAGLE OWL

TASSLED SCORPIONFISH

GREEN SPIDER

HIDDEN ANIMALS CAMOUFLAGE

Is this hiker on the verge of toppling off a cliff into a deep canyon? If you said yes, the optical illusion fooled you! This is no cliffhanger. The hiker is actually walking safely along the edge of a pool of water in Glen Canyon National Recreation Area in Utah, U.S.A. The canyon walls above the hiker are reflected in the water. *Whew!* For more about this optical illusion, turn to page 46.

TAKE A **LOOK!** UNDER THE SEA

Fun Fact!

Detached **sea star arms** can sometimes grow **new bodies.**

< FIND THESE OBJECTS IN THE SEA. >

2 anchors

7 sea stars

2 hammerhead sharks

1 moray eel

6 seashells

1 sea turtle

5 clownfish

3 seahorses

2 lobsters

2 diving flippers

MORE CHALLENGES

IF YOU'RE READY FOR THE NEXT LEVEL of brain-boggling puzzles, you're in the right place! You can turn the games you've already completed into new challenges using the tips in this section, or create your own puzzles at home to stump your friends and family. There's no reason the fun has to end just because the book does!

WHAT IN THE REAL WORLD?

The up-close images in the "What in the World?" games challenge our brains to use clues to solve puzzles and think in a different way. Try these variations to stretch your thinking.

Bird's-eye View: pages 6–7
- While you're looking at a magazine or surfing online, start to notice the distance and angle from which photographs were taken. Think about different ways the photographer might have shot the same subject.
- Use your imagination to think of how various scenes might look from an airplane. Draw a picture of what you're imagining.

Look Up: pages 18–19
- Go outdoors for this challenge. Visit a park or go to your own backyard. What do you see in the sky when you look up at different times of day? Make a list.
- Now think about what you *don't* see. Imagine what it would be like to see unusual things in the sky above you. List all of the things you *wish* you could see in the sky when you look up.

Yellows: pages 32–33
- All of the objects are shades of yellow. How many other yellow things can you name?
- Try the same game with other colors.

REAL OR FAKE?

Today's advanced technology makes it pretty easy to take a photograph of something that never happened or doesn't really exist. And with easy access to all of the information out there on the Internet, it's even easier to believe it! Practice refining your detective skills with these tips and tricks:

- Ask questions: Does the photo look too unbelievable? Do you think it's possible to accomplish the feat shown in the image? Where could the picture have been taken? If it seems impossible, it just might be.
- Look for telltale signs of digital alterations. Is the horizon even? Do the borders match up? Is there a mistake the digital artist didn't catch?
- Search the Web for the truth. Enlist the help of an adult to do a quick search on questionable photos. There are plenty of sources doing research on hoaxes that can give you the full answer.
- Go with your gut. Usually your first instinct is correct. If something feels wrong, it probably is.

TAKE ANOTHER LOOK!

There's much more to discover in these puzzles! Here's a list of some ways to test your powers of observation:

Galápagos Islands: pages 10–11
- Do some research about the unique birds found in the Galápagos Islands and identify six different bird species in the scene.
- Which animals have flippers and which have feet?
- How many different types of crabs can you find?
- Identify all of the objects that were made by humans.

Barnyard: pages 20–21
- Count the number of mammals versus the number of birds in the scene.
- Which animals have horns?
- Identify all of the farm tools.
- How many animals are not standing on the ground?
- Do you see a pig doing something funny in the picture?

The Circus: pages 28–29
- Find everything that has wheels.
- Count all of the balloons, including the hot-air balloons on the Ferris wheel.
- How many people can you see, and what are they doing?
- Which items in the scene are round?
- What can you eat or drink at the circus?

Under the Sea: pages 38–39
- Find all of the blue creatures in the picture.
- How many different kinds of coral do you see?
- Can you find a school of small white fish?
- Count the number of striped fishes in the scene.

- Imagine you are the diver in the picture. Draw what you would like to see if you had an underwater perspective.

UP CLOSE—GET EVEN CLOSER!

You may be surprised by what you see when you use a magnifying glass to look at a pinecone, a butterfly's wing, your lunch, or anything else that interests you! Here are some fun ways you can get an up-close view of everyday items:

- Grab a magnifying glass to become a micro detective. How close can you get and what can you see?
- If you have access to a microscope, you're in for a treat! Put everyday objects under the micro-scope and check them out. Some ideas to get you started: a grain of rice, a worm, your pet's hair, a flower petal, a dead bug, a drop of pond water. How do the views differ from what you can see with your naked eye?
- Make drawings of the magnified images you see and ask friends if they can identify them.
- Search online for scanning electron microscope (SEM) photographs that will reveal amazing details of animals, plants, and objects.

MORE CHALLENGES

SPOTTING HIDDEN ANIMALS

There are hidden animals all around you, whether you live in a city or in the country. Often you don't notice them because they're hiding or blend in with their surroundings. But you can see many things if you look around and remain quiet when you're outside. Here's how to improve your observation and visual discrimination skills while watching animals in their natural habitats. Caution: Be sure to keep your distance from wild animals!

- Sit quietly and observe your surroundings. You can do this anywhere—in your backyard, a park, forest, desert, or beach.
- After five minutes, write down some details you didn't notice earlier.
- How many different plants and animals did you notice around you? Look closely so you observe even the smallest insects.
- Snap a photo! Try photographing an animal or insect from various angles to capture the best light and perspective.

SEEING OPTICAL ILLUSIONS IN NATURE

Optical illusions are all around you—it's simply a matter of training your brain to see them. Here are some tips for how to become more aware of optical illusions in the natural world.

- When you're outdoors, take in the entire scene. Some people tend to focus only on one thing, and they miss the big picture. When you start to notice the interesting pattern on the tree bark, maybe you can see that there's a spider hiding there!
- Remember that a lot of insects and animals mimic other things. Stay alert to movement when you're in nature. You may see a stick walk away, or a thorn on a stem change positions.
- Shadows and perspective make great optical illusions. Start noticing patterns that different objects create with their shadows. Look at the same shadows at different times of day. How have they changed?
- Have you ever taken a photograph and noticed something when you looked at it later that you didn't see when you snapped the picture? Start scrutinizing the foreground and background of your photos to see what you may be missing in real life.

DOUBLE TAKE TWO

Want to quiz your friends and fool your family with more puzzles like the "Double Take" games in this book? Try these activities in a group:

- 🔆 For a short-term memory workout, go back to the coral reef photographs on pages 16–17. Spend a few minutes finding the differences between the two images. Then close the book and write down as many of the differences as you can remember. Repeat the exercise using the images on pages 30–31.

- 🔆 For a long-term memory test, do the same exercise as above, but look at the photographs in the morning and wait until evening—or the next day—to write the list. Try it again a week later and see if your memory improved.

- 🔆 Now use the pictures to test how observant you are. Study one of the pictures for a few minutes, and then close the book. Describe specific details of the photograph to a friend. How did you do?

- 🔆 Take a picture of an ordinary scene such as your room, your backyard, or a park. Change ten things and reshoot the photograph. Print both pictures and lay them side by side. See if your friends and family can spot the differences!

- 🔆 Practice doing picture puzzles with a timer to increase your brain's processing speed.

SHHH! ANSWERS

TITLE PAGE
(pages 2–3)

An elephant hawk moth's brilliant colors blend in with fall foliage. The "elephant" part of its name comes from its caterpillar stage, when it has a retractable trunk-like appendage on its head.

WHAT IN THE WORLD?
(pages 6–7)

Top row: flamingos, camels, island, forest, coral reef. **Bottom row:** hot-air balloon, icebergs, elephants, tulip fields.

REAL OR FAKE?
(pages 8–9)

1. real, 2. fake, 3. real, 4. real

TAKE A LOOK!
(pages 10–11)

UP CLOSE
(pages 12–13)

1. damselfly, 2. chameleon, 3. crowned crane, 4. moth caterpillar, 5. pinecone, 6. snowflake

HIDDEN ANIMALS
(page 14)

FROGFISH

LEAF BUTTERFLY

SEAHORSE

LICHEN SPIDER

FROG HAWKSBILL TURTLE

OPTICAL ILLUSION
(page 15)

Illusion explained: When you cover the zebra head on the right it's easier to see that the zebra facing left is the one whose body is in the center foreground. Now cover the left head. Do you see that the body on the left side belongs to the right-facing zebra, which is standing slightly behind the other? Zebras hang in herds, and all those stripes are confusing! The stripes actually help protect zebras in the wild because this tricky illusion, called "disruptive camouflage," confuses predators. It's hard for a lion to single out one zebra in the crowd, so they can hide in plain sight!

DOUBLE TAKE
(pages 16–17)

WHAT IN THE WORLD?
(pages 18–19)

Top row: northern lights, ladybug, kite, bat.
Bottom row: fireworks, hang glider, macaw, space station.

TAKE A LOOK!
(pages 20–21)

REAL OR FAKE?
(pages 22–23)

1. fake, 2. real, 3. real, 4. real

UP CLOSE
(pages 24–25)

1. pheasant, 2. snow peas, 3. elephant, 4. morpho butterfly, 5. green tree python, 6. sea star

HIDDEN ANIMALS
(page 26)

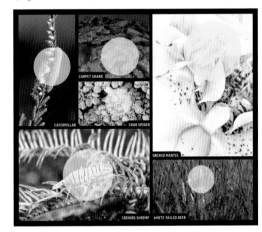

OPTICAL ILLUSION
(page 27)

Illusion explained: It's just a reflection—not two turtles playing piggyback! The phenomenon that causes this effect, called "total internal reflection," is created by the angle of the light as it travels up through the water. At the ocean's surface, light rays change direction at a certain angle, which creates a mirror effect. To use this concept to make creative photos, underwater photographers look for calm, smooth water and a subject—such as a turtle—near the surface.

TAKE A LOOK!
(pages 28–29)

DOUBLE TAKE
(pages 30–31)

WHAT IN THE WORLD?
(pages 32–33)

Top row: honeycomb, tennis ball, butterfly, snake, corn. **Bottom row:** slug, canary, lemon, sunflowers.

45

SHHH! ANSWERS

REAL OR FAKE?
(pages 34–35)

1. real, 2. real, 3. fake, 4. real

HIDDEN ANIMALS
(page 36)

OPTICAL ILLUSION
(page 37)

Illusion explained: What appears to be a precarious situation for the hiker in Glen Canyon National Recreation Area in Utah is actually quite safe. The hiker is walking along the edge of a pool of water. The canyon is behind him, reflected on the smooth surface of the pool. This tricky pic was achieved by capturing the reflection and the hiker's shadow at exactly the right moment. Mirrors and other reflective surfaces like water are excellent ways to create optical illusions, which is why magicians often use them to amaze their audiences!

TAKE A LOOK!
(pages 38–39)

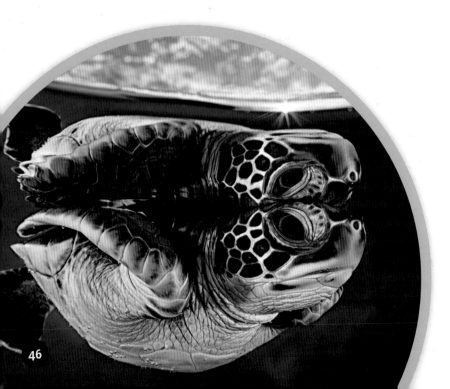

Fun Fact! **Thirsty?** Your **brain** is about **three-quarters water.**

MORE TO EXPLORE

HAVE FUN EXPLORING more optical illusions, puzzles, and games with these websites, books, and other resources.

WEBSITES

kids.nationalgeographic.com
This site inspires curious kids and makes learning fun. Check out the games section!

kids.niehs.nih.gov/index.htm
Discover tons of games at this "Kids' Pages" site from the National Institute of Environmental Health Sciences.

kidskonnect.com
A safe Internet gateway that is loaded with brain games just for kids.

lumosity.com
A website where people of all ages can build a personalized brain-training program.

BOOKS & MAGAZINES

Xtreme Illusions* and *Xtreme Illusions 2
National Geographic Kids Books, 2012 and 2014
Mind-bending collections of visual puzzles that will amaze your friends, mystify your family, and blow your own mind!

The Big Book of Fun!
National Geographic Kids Books, 2010
Check out these boredom-busting games, jokes, puzzles, mazes, and more!

Complete Guide to Brain Health
By Michael S. Sweeney
National Geographic Books, 2013
A book for the whole family to learn simple exercises that can strengthen your brain.

Brain Games
By Jennifer Swanson
National Geographic Kids Books, 2015
Time to exercise your noggin and have a blast doing it. A superfun compilation of challenges, myths, fun facts, science, and games all about your brain!

Brainworks
By Michael S. Sweeney
National Geographic Books, 2011
This book for adults and kids reveals the mind-bending science of how you see, what you think, and who you are. Includes cool optical illusions.

Mastermind
By Stephanie Drimmer
National Geographic Kids Books, 2015
Test your smarts with interactive puzzles and games, and learn how to unleash your inner genius.

***National Geographic Kids* magazine**
Dare to explore! Look for visual games and activities in the "Fun Stuff" department.

TELEVISION

Grab a parent and tune in to ***Brain Games*** on the National Geographic Channel.
Parents: **braingames.nationalgeographic.com**

CREDITS

Art directed by Callie Broaddus
Designed by Stephanie White

Printed in China
16/PPS/1

ILLUSTRATIONS

"Look" illustrations by Damien Vignaux, colagene.com

Photo editing by Erin West Kephart; **FRONT COVER:** (background), Edwin Verin/Dreamstime.com; (UP LE), Gillian Plummer/Flowerphotos/ARDEA; (UP RT), Tsekhmister/Dreamstime.com; (UP CTR RT), Colin Marshall/ARDEA; (LO RT), Kondor83/Shutterstock; **SPINE:** Paul Williams—Funkystock/imageBROKER/Corbis; **BACK COVER:** Caters/ZUMA Press/Newscom; 1 (UP LE), Constantinos Petrinos/Minden Pictures; 1, (UP CTR), amana images inc./Alamy Stock Photo; 1 (UP RT), Jeff R Clow/Getty Images; 1 (CTR LE), Jurgen Freund/Nature Picture Library; 1 (CTR), Christian Ziegler/National Geographic Creative; 1 (CTR RT), Rudi Von Briel/Getty Images; 1 (LO LE), Fred Hirschmann/Science Faction/Getty Images; 1 (LO CTR), Alex Hyde/Nature Picture Library; 1 (LO RT), Alex Hyde/Nature Picture Library; 2-3, Victor Savushkin/Alamy Stock Photo; 4 (CTR), Eddie Gerald; 4 (UP RT), Colin Hutton; 4 (LO RT), Digitally composed artwork by Damien Vignaux; 5 (UP), Alex Hyde/Nature Picture Library; 5 (CTR LE), Constantinos Petrinos/Minden Pictures; 5 (LO), Emily Mitchell/National Geographic Creative; 5 (CTR RT), Constantinos Petrinos/Minden Pictures; 6, Richard du Toit Photography; 7 (UP LE), Firefly Productions/Corbis; 7 (UP CTR LE), Ira Block/National Geographic Creative; 7 (UP CTR RT), Carr Clifton/Minden Pictures; 7 (UP RT), Eddie Gerald; 7 (LO LE), Philip Wallick/Corbis; 7 (LO CTR LE), Fred Hirschmann/Science Faction/Getty Images; 7 (LO CTR RT), imageBROKER/Alamy Stock Photo; 7 (LO RT), Frans Lemmens/Getty Images; 8 (LE), Colin Hutton; 8 (UP RT), paytai/Shutterstock; 8 (UP CTR RT), Stacey Ann Alberts/Shutterstock; 8 (LO RT), Papilio/Alamy Stock Photo; 9, The Africa Image Library/Alamy Stock Photo; 10-11, Digitally composed artwork by Damien Vignaux; 11 (UP), David Fleetham/Alamy Stock Photo; 12 (UP LE), Murray Clarke/Alamy Stock Photo; 12 (UP CTR), Alex Hyde/Nature Picture Library; 12 (UP RT), Edwin Giesbers/Nature Picture Library; 12 (LO LE), Cathy Keifer/Dreamstime.com; 12 (LO CTR), Jefunne/Shutterstock; 12 (LO RT), Jinfeng Zhang/Dreamstime.com; 13 (UP LE), Ingo Arndt/Minden Pictures; 13 (UP CTR), Shutterstock; 13 (UP RT), MarcelClemens/Shutterstock; 13 (LO LE), Raymond B. Summers/Dreamstime.com; 13 (LO CTR), Nico Smit/Dreamstime.com; 13 (LO RT), Sailorr/Dreamstime.com; 14 (UP LE), Premaphotos/Minden Pictures; 14 (UP CTR), Nature Picture Library/Alamy Stock Photo; 14 (UP RT), Doug Perrine/Minden Pictures; 14 (CTR RT), Jurgen Freund/Nature Picture Library; 14 (LO LE), Inaki Relanzon/Minden Pictures; 14 (LO RT), Jurgen Freund/Minden Pictures; 15, Emily Mitchell/National Geographic Creative; 16-17, Constantinos Petrinos/Minden Pictures; 17 (UP LE), Richard Carey/Dreamstime.com; 17 (UP RT), Rich Carey/Shutterstock; 17 (CTR LE), Bluehand/Dreamstime.com; 17 (CTR), Cigdem Sean Cooper/Dreamstime.com; 17 (CTR RT), Richard Carey/Dreamstime.com; 17 (LO LE), Cigdem Sean Cooper/Shutterstock; 17 (LO CTR), Alexchered/Dreamstime.com; 18, Noppawat Tom Charoensinphon/Getty Images; 19 (UP LE), Stephen Dalton/Minden Pictures; 19 (UP CTR LE), Mark Bassett/Alamy; 19 (UP CTR RT), Tom Grill/Getty Images; 19 (UP RT), Thomas Marent/Minden Pictures; 19 (LO LE), Rudi Von Briel/Getty Images; 19 (LO CTR LE), Nigel Hicks/Alamy; 19 (LO CTR RT), Mint Images/Art Wolfe/Getty Images; 19 (LO RT), NASA; 20-21, Digitally composed artwork by Damien Vignaux; 21 (UP), Congressional Quarterly/CQ Roll Call/Newscom; 22 (UP LE), Marina Yamkovskaia/Caters News Agency; 22 (LO LE), WENN Ltd/Alamy Stock Photo; 22 (RT), Keren Su/Corbis; 23, Christian Ziegler/National Geographic Creative; 24 (UP LE), Alex Hyde/Nature Picture Library; 24 (UP CTR), Alwyn J Roberts/Minden Pictures; 24 (UP RT), jeep2499/Shutterstock; 24 (LO LE), Johnbell/Dreamstime.com; 24 (LO CTR), Danita Delimont/Alamy Stock Photo; 24 (LO RT), Matt May/Alamy Stock Photo; 25 (UP LE), Jerzy Gubernator/Science Source; 25 (UP CTR), Amwu/Dreamstime.com; 25 (UP RT), Vilainecrevette/Alamy Stock Photo; 25 (LO LE), Kooslin/Dreamstime.com; 25 (LO CTR), Deaddogdodge/Dreamstime.com; 25 (LO RT), Duncan Noakes/Dreamstime.com; 26 (UP LE), Derek Middleton/Minden Pictures; 26 (UP CTR), Doug Perrine/Minden Pictures; 26 (CTR), Tom Murphy/Getty Images; 26 (UP RT), Alex Hyde/Nature Picture Library; 26 (LO LE), Constantinos Petrinos/Minden Pictures; 26 (LO RT), Jim Brandenburg/National Geographic Creative; 27, Jordi Chias/Nature Picture Library; 28-29, Digitally composed artwork by Damien Vignaux; 29 (UP), Volodymyr Kyrylyuk/Dreamstime.com; 30-31, Sergei Kazakov/Shutterstock; 31 (UP LE), Dmitri Pravdjukov/Dreamstime.com; 31 (UP), Snicol24/Dreamstime.com; 31 (UP RT), Kostiuchenko/Dreamstime.com; 31 (LO CTR), Ncristian/Dreamstime.com; 31 (LO RT), Ivonne Wierink/Dreamstime.com; 32, amana images inc./Alamy Stock Photo; 33 (UP LE), Stockbyte/Getty Images; 33 (UP CTR LE), Charles Smith/Corbis; 33 (UP CTR RT), George Grall/National Geographic Creative; 33 (UP RT), RBP Trust/Getty Images; 33 (LO LE), Ed Reschke/Getty Images; 33 (LO CTR LE), ARCO/Nature Picture Library; 33 (LO CTR RT), Francesco Ruggeri/Getty Images; 33 (LO RT), Ed Collacott/Getty Images; 34 (UP LE), Oliver Richter; 34 (LO LE), Paul Mayall Wildlife/Alamy Stock Photo; 34 (LO CTR LE), Vinai Thongumpai/Dreamstime.com; 34 (RT), Reuters/Daniel Munoz; 35, Paula Hammack; 36 (UP LE), Tom Mangelsen/Minden Pictures; 36 (UP CTR), Pascal Kobeh/Nature Picture Library; 36 (CTR), Jeff R Clow/Getty Images; 36 (UP RT), Michel Poinsignon/Minden Pictures; 36 (LO LE), Georgette Douwma/Minden Pictures; 36 (LO RT), Thomas Marent/Minden Pictures; 37, Darrell Staggs/Caters News Agency; 38-39, Digitally composed artwork by Damien Vignaux; 39 (UP), Brandon Cole Marine Photography/Alamy Stock Photo; 40 (UP), Christian Ziegler/National Geographic Creative; 40 (LO), Frans Lemmens/Getty Images; 41 (UP), Digitally composed artwork by Damien Vignaux; 41 (LO), Ingo Arndt/Minden Pictures; 42 (UP), Darrell Staggs/Caters News Agency; 42 (LO), Inaki Relanzon/Minden Pictures; 43, Sergei Kazakov/Shutterstock; 46 (LO LE), Jordi Chias/Nature Picture Library; 47, Nico Smit/Dreamstime.com